D0824633

Games Around the World

Spinning Toys

by Dana Meachen Rau

Content Adviser: Mats Selen, Ph.D., Department of Physics, University of Illinois
Reading Adviser: Rosemary G. Palmer, Ph.D., Department of Literacy,
College of Education, Boise State University

COMPASS POINT BOOKS  MINNEAPOLIS, MINNESOTA

Compass Point Books
3109 West 50th Street, #115
Minneapolis, MN 55410

Visit Compass Point Books on the Internet at www.compasspointbooks.com
or e-mail your request to custserv@compasspointbooks.com

Photographs ©: Gary Sundermeyer, cover; Phil Mislinski/Getty Images, 4;
Gianni Dagli Orti/Corbis, 6; Mary Evans Picture Library, 7, 8; Tops from
the Judith Schulz Collection, Spinning Top Museum, Burlington,
Wisconsin, USA, 9, 10 (all), 11; Scala/Art Resource, N.Y., 17; Special
Collections, The University of Arizona Library, 19; Paul A. Souders/Corbis,
26; BananaStock, 27.

Creative Director: Terri Foley
Managing Editor: Catherine Neitge
Editor: Jennifer VanVoorst
Photo Researcher: Svetlana Zhurkina
Designer/Page production: Bradfordesign, Inc./Jaime Martens
Illustrator: Claudia Wolf
Educational Consultant: Diane Smolinski

Library of Congress Cataloging-in-Publication Data
Rau, Dana Meachen, 1971–
    Spinning toys / by Dana Meachen Rau.
      p. cm. — (Games around the world)
    Includes bibliographical references and index.
    ISBN 0-7565-0676-X (hardcover)
      1. Tops—Juvenile literature. 2. Flying discs (Game)—
      Juvenile literature. [1. Tops. 2. Flying discs (Game) 3. Toys.
      4. Games.] I. Title. II. Series.
GV1218.T5R39 2005
796.2—dc22   2003024095

Table of Contents

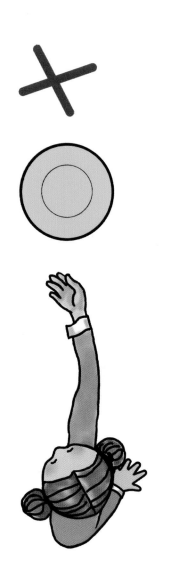

NOTE: *In this book, words that are defined in the glossary are in* **bold** *the first time they appear in the text.*

Feeling Dizzy!

Do you like to spread out your arms and spin in a circle? Spinning can make you feel very dizzy! Did you know that even when you are not playing a spinning game, you are still spinning? In fact, you are spinning all of the time. This is because you live on Earth. The planet Earth is always spinning in space.

Throughout history, people have been interested in objects that spin. People have made and played with spinning toys and created games around their use. There are two types of spinning toys that people play with all over the world. They are spinning tops and flying discs. Tops spin on the ground. Discs spin through the air. Unlike people, however, tops and discs never get dizzy!

◀ *People around the world enjoy games using flying discs.*

The History of Tops

People in many ancient cultures played with tops. Vases, sculptures, and carvings from ancient civilizations show pictures of people spinning tops.

Top spinning, or *koma asobi*, has always been very popular in Japan. Tops first came to Japan from China about 1,200 years ago. They were not children's toys. Only very wealthy people played with tops.

6 ▲ *A carving from ancient Turkey shows two men playing with a top.*

By the mid-1800s in Japan, spinning tops had ▶ *become almost purely a children's game.*

Tops were also a fun pastime in Europe. In the Middle Ages, tops were called prills, spilcocks, or whirligigs. In the late 1800s, children held contests to see whose top could spin the longest, or if one top could knock another one down.

▲ *Contests with tops were popular in the late 1800s.*

Tops were made from whatever material was available where a person lived. The earliest tops may have been made from nuts. People who lived near the sea made their tops from shells. In China, people made tops from **bamboo.** Tops have been made of rocks, wood, metal, and plastic, and are sometimes painted with colors and designs.

How to Spin a Top

There are different kinds of tops. You spin each type in a different way.

A hand-spun top usually has a stem sticking out of its tip. You start the top by quickly turning the stem between your thumb and first finger. Some tops with long stems can be started by rubbing the stem between your two hands.

▲ *These hand-spun tops are made of wood, plastic, and metal.*

9

A peg top is started
by pulling a string. The
string is wound tightly
around the top. You
throw the top to the
ground while pulling
on the string.

A whip top is started
by hand or by a string.
Then, to keep it moving,
it is hit with a whip.
Whip tops are the type
used by many
ancient cultures.

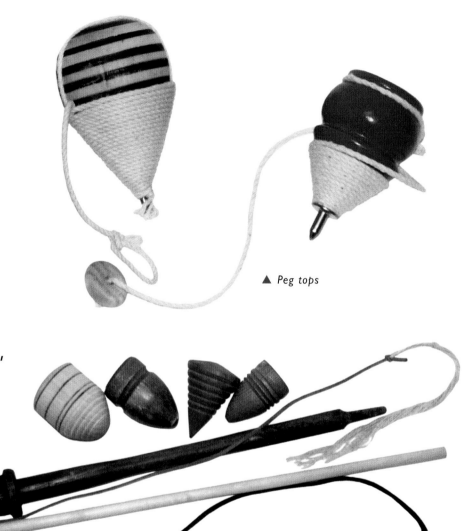

▲ Peg tops

▲ Whip tops and whips

10

Another kind of top has a spring inside. This type of top may be started by winding the spring tight with a key and then letting it go. Sometimes you may pump a handle on the top up and down to get the top moving.

▲ *Pump-handled top*

Listening to tops can be as fun as spinning them! Holes cut into the sides of some tops can create a humming or whistling sound when the tops are spun.

11

How to Make a Top

You can make your own hand-spun top!

What you need: A plastic lid (from a margarine container, yogurt container, coffee can, etc.), a ruler, a nail, a sharpened pencil, rubber bands, and decorations (permanent markers and/or stickers)

1. Find the exact center of the lid. You can do this by measuring across the lid in two places with a ruler and marking the center.

2. Then poke a hole through the center of the lid with the nail.

▲ *Use a ruler to find the center of the lid.*

3. Slide the pencil through the hole in the lid. The hole should be just big enough for the pencil to fit very tightly.

4. Wind rubber bands around the pencil both above and below the lid. Push the rubber bands as close to the lid as possible. (This will keep the lid still as it spins.)

5. Decorate your top, if you wish, with colorful designs.

▲ *Push the pencil through the hole in the lid and wrap both sides of the pencil with rubber bands.*

6. Find a flat surface and spin the stem of your top between your thumb and first finger or between your hands.

7. See how long your top can spin! Also, watch how your decorations change as the top spins.

▲ *Spin the stem of your top between your thumb and first finger.*

The Dreidel Game

A dreidel (pronounced DRAY-dl) is a type of hand-spun top. It has four flat sides, each of which shows a **Hebrew** letter. The game of dreidel has been played for thousands of years.

Here's how to play:

- Sit at a table with two or more players.

- In the center of the table, place a bowl filled with small objects. These could be candy, peanuts, buttons, or pennies.

- Take turns spinning the dreidel. Watch to see which letter faces up when the dreidel lands.

נ *Nun* means you do not get to take any objects from the bowl.

ג *Gimel* means you can take all of the objects from the bowl.

ה *Hay* means you can take half of the objects from the bowl.

שׁ *Shin* means you have to put one of your objects back into the bowl.

- The game is over when one player has all the objects. This player is the winner! (If only one object or no objects are left in the bowl and there is no winner yet, each player must return one item to the bowl and continue until someone wins.)

The History of Discs

People in ancient cultures also enjoyed tossing discs through the air. **Discus** throwing was one of the events at the first **Olympic Games** in 776 B.C. A discus was a round, flat disc made of heavy bronze or iron. The person who could throw the discus the farthest won the event.

Discs were not only used in sports. They were also used as weapons. Ancient Roman soldiers threw their round **shields** in battle, and in India in the 1400s, soldiers threw sharp, flat rings called *chacarani.*

▲ *This statue shows a Greek discus thrower from the fifth century B.C.*

17

All over Europe, spinning disc games developed. Quoits was a popular game in Scotland and England in the 1300s. Players threw a ring or disc and tried to get it on or near a peg in the ground. Quoits is like the game of horseshoes today.

Native Americans also had spinning disc and ring games. The Native Americans made hoops out of bark or thin wood. They would try to throw their spears through these hoops as the hoops rolled along the ground. In another game, they threw rings in the air and tried to catch them on their spears.

In the early 1900s, throwing pie tins and cookie tin lids became a fun game that people played in parks, in their backyards, or during recess. In the mid-1950s, discs began to be made out of plastic. Plastic discs could fly farther and be thrown with greater accuracy than pie plates. This is the type of flying disc people play with today.

University students played with flying discs in the 1970s. ▶

How to Throw a Disc

There are many ways to throw a disc, but the backhand throw will make your disc fly far and straight.

▲ *How to hold a disc*

- If you are right-handed, stand so that your **target** is to your right. (If you are left-handed, it should be to your left.)

- Hold the disc by its edge, with your thumb on top and your other fingers underneath.

- Pull your arm across your chest.

▲ *Pull your arm across your chest.*

- Quickly fling your arm toward your target.

- At the moment your arm is straight out at your side, flick your wrist and let go of the disc.

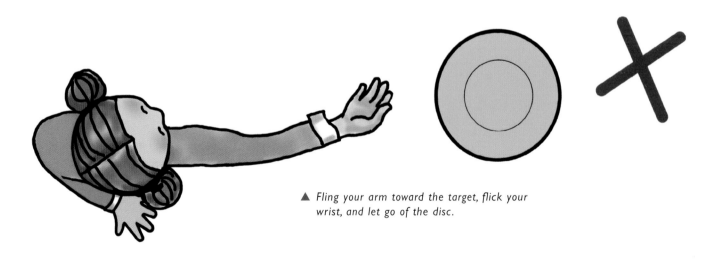

▲ *Fling your arm toward the target, flick your wrist, and let go of the disc.*

Disc Bowling

Bowling games have been played in many countries throughout history. In the 1300s in China, people played a game called quills. British people in the 1800s played a game called skittles. Sometimes they played skittles inside using small wooden pins. A spinning top knocked them down. Sometimes they played with larger pins outdoors, on the grass or even on ice. The pins were knocked down by throwing a wooden disc at them.

Disc bowling games are a fun way to play with your flying disc.

Here's one way to play:

- First you need 10 pins. These can be any objects that resemble bowling pins. Tall plastic cups, cardboard tubes, or empty soda or water bottles work well.

- Set up the pins outside with one pin in the first row, two in the second, three in the third, and four in the fourth.

- Stand about 75 feet (23 meters) away from the pins.

- Throw your disc at the pins and see how many you can knock down. You have two tries to knock down all 10.

You can also play disc bowling inside. Instead of throwing the disc at the pins, you can slide the disc along the ground.

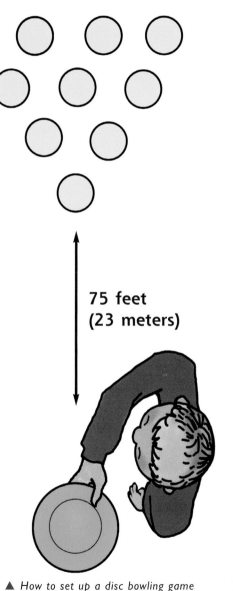

75 feet (23 meters)

▲ *How to set up a disc bowling game*

23

Ultimate

Ultimate is a sport that was invented by high school students in 1967. The object of the game is to score points by catching the disc within the goal line of the other team.

- Teams can have from three to 12 players.

- Each team lines up along its goal line. The team with the disc throws it to the other team.

- The disc is thrown, or passed, from player to player down the field, much as the ball is passed in the game of soccer.

- When a team catches the disc within the other team's goal line, that team gets a point.

- Players cannot run with the disc. Once they catch it, they have to throw it within 10 seconds.

- If one team drops the disc or doesn't complete a pass, or if the pass is blocked by the other team, the other team gets the disc.

- Players cannot touch each other during a game.

- There are no **referees.** Players are expected to play fair on their own.

The Ultimate playing field

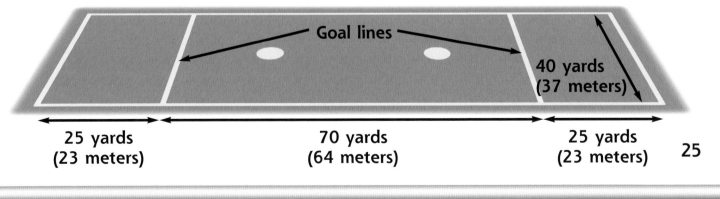

Goal lines

40 yards
(37 meters)

25 yards
(23 meters)

70 yards
(64 meters)

25 yards
(23 meters)

All Kinds of Spinning

All over the world, you will find children enjoying spinning toys. They might be playing with tops on the pavement or throwing discs in a field. They might be blowing into a pinwheel or trying to keep a hula hoop on their waist. They could be riding a bike with spinning wheels. So many fun things to do include spinning!

Next time you spin a top or toss a disc, remember that you are sharing a pastime with people everywhere. They are enjoying spinning just like you.

▲ *A boy plays with a peg top in Jerusalem, Israel.*

You can enjoy spinning when you ride your bike! ▶

Glossary

bamboo—a grass with hard, hollow stems

discus—a round, flat, heavy disc usually made of metal

Hebrew—the language Jewish people speak in Israel and all Jews use in prayers

Olympic Games—a gathering held every four years in which athletes from many countries compete against one another

referees—officials who make sure players follow the rules of the game

shields—large discs of metal or wood that soldiers used to block arrows or spears

target—the spot at which someone is aiming

Did You Know?

 Historians can tell where tops from ancient Japan were made. Tops were painted in colors specific to certain regions of the country.

 A diabolo is an hourglass-shaped top used by jugglers. It is tossed into the air, instead of on the ground, to spin. It is then caught with a rope and tossed again.

 Tippe tops are an interesting type of hand-spun top. They start to spin and then flip over and continue to spin on their stems.

 The Maori people of New Zealand play with a top called a *potaka.* Both ends of a potaka are pointed. They whip it while it is spinning so it flips from one end to the other.

 One type of Japanese top is called the *narigomal,* or "crying top." It has a small hole in the side that makes a crying noise when spun.

 The pie tins from The Frisbie Baking Company in Bridgeport, Connecticut, were some of the ones that made throwing discs a favorite pastime.

 There are lots of clubs for dogs and their owners who play flying disc games together. There are even world championship tournaments where dogs can show off their skills.

 Disc golf is a fun sport in which players throw a disc through a course, trying to hit a target on each "hole."

 People buy a lot of basketballs, footballs, and baseballs every year, but they buy more flying discs than all of those balls added together.

Want to Know More?

At the Library

Hindley, Judy. *The Wheeling and Whirling-Around Book*. Boston: Candlewick Press, 1994.

Malafronte, Victor A. *The Complete Book of Frisbee*. Alameda, Calif.: American Trends Publishing Co., 1998.

Wiese, Jim. *Rocket Science: 50 Flying, Floating, Flipping, Spinning Gadgets Kids Create Themselves*. New York: Wiley, 1995.

On the Web

For more information on spinning toys, use FactHound to track down Web sites related to this book.

1. Go to *www.facthound.com*
2. Type in a search word related to this book or this book ID: 075650676X
3. Click on the *Fetch It* button.

Your trusty FactHound will fetch the best Web sites for you!

On the Road

The Spinning Top Museum
533 Milwaukee Ave.
Burlington, WI
414/763-3946
To see more than 2,000 tops and other spinning toys

The Strong Museum's National Toy Hall of Fame
1 Manhattan Square
Rochester, NY 14607
585/263-2700
To see a collection of important historical toys, including flying discs

Index

About the Author

Dana Meachen Rau is an author, editor, and illustrator.
A graduate of Trinity College in Hartford, Connecticut,
she has written more than 90 books for children,
including nonfiction, biographies, early readers,
and historical fiction. Ms. Rau loves to play games.
She plays with tops and discs in Burlington,
Connecticut, with her husband, Chris, and children,
Charlie and Allison.